TO DAD

Laura Brydon   Age 7

A gift book written by children for fathers everywhere

Edited by Richard & Helen Exley

⧉EXLEY

To Lincoln and Dalton

Emma Dallas   Age 9

First edition published in Great Britain
in 1976, revised and updated in 1990 by
Exley Publications Ltd.
Copyright © Richard and Helen Exley,
1976 and 1990
ISBN 1-85015-222-5
Second edition published in
Great Britain in 1990
Published simultaneously in 1992 by
Exley Publications in Great Britain,
and Exley Giftbooks in the USA.
A copy of the CIP data is available from the
British Library on request. All rights reserved.
No part of this publication may be reproduced
or transmitted in any form or by any means,
electronic or mechanical, including photocopy,
recording or any information storage and
retrieval system without permission in writing
from the Publisher.
Front cover illustration by Katy Low
Back cover illustration by Laura Depiano, age 5

Exley Publications Ltd, 16 Chalk Hill, Watford,
Herts WD1 4BN, United Kingdom
Exley Giftbooks, 359 East Main Street, Suite 3D,
Mount Kisco, NY 10549, USA.

PRINTING HISTORY
First edition *1976*
Second printing 1976
Third printing 1977
Fourth printing 1978
Fifth printing 1978
Sixth printing 1980
Seventh printing 1981
Eighth printing 1981
Ninth printing 1982
Tenth printing 1983
Eleventh printing 1984
Twelfth printing 1985
Thirteenth printing 1986
Fourteenth printing 1989
Fifteenth printing 1990

Second edition *1990*
First printing 1990
Second printing 1991
Third printing 1992
Fourth printing 1992
Fifth printing 1992
Sixth printing 1993

Printed and bound in Hungary.

All shapes and sizes

Dads wear socks so that We can not see there hairre legs.

Sara Beesley

Dad's wear wig's to hide there tatty hair.

Sean   Age 8

My dad often wears a yukky green sweater with holes in the elbows. He says that these holes are there so that his elbows can breathe.

Rebecca Skett   Age 11

My father likes comfortable clothes, like old corduroys and flannel shirts, they look a bit messy though, so we have to dress him up in respectable clothes.

Emma   Age 10

My dad is tall and large out ways. His eyes are popping out but when he is happy they go back in his head.

Helen Francis   age 7

My dad is nearly six foot three.
He's lot more bigger than you.

David Burkey

Karen Murray
Age 10

Neil King
Age 9

David Royffe

Some are big and strong,
Some are small and fat
Some are thin and some are thick
What funny dads we've got!

Janice Jones

My dad is a bit bald,
My dad is fat,
My dad isn't old
Well not quite yet.

Jane   Age 11

Dad has got a sweet tooth,
And I mean a sweet *tooth*
He's had all the rest pulled out!

Lisa   Age 10

Brigitte Corbett   Age 6

Paul Lowe   Age 7

Christopher
Pearson
Age 8

Victoria

9

A father is a man mother but unlike a mother he is not always on the telephone.

Clare Dawkins

Only a father would ride on the roller coaster with me, come off with a green face and say he had a good time.

Loni Casale   Age 11

In the crazy world of television, people seem to think that dads are funny things that live in paint-pots and jump up and down on the best dining-room table singing about Birdseye puddings. In fact they are not. They are really perfectly sane things that would spank you if you tried to do the same.

Guy Hannaford

My dad watches Kojak and Cannon because they are more bald and fat than he is.

Mark Wickham-Jones   Age 13

A dad is a person who is hiding behind the newspapers every Sunday.

Wendy

Mothers wear dresses to cuver theer panties and bras. Dads wear long pants to cuver theer underpants.

Timothy

When my dad comes in from work the house fills with laughter.

Thomas Telford   Age 11

Dads have a pretty fundamental place in the hearts of their children, as this new edition of TO DAD shows very clearly. Kids may take the mickey out of Dad, but the love remains strong, and it shows even in the funniest entries. Dads are fun to be with, and love being laughed at and laughed with.

TO DAD was originally created in the 1970s, from entries sent in from schools all over the world – Britain, the United States, Australia, New Zealand, Jamaica, Denmark, Germany, Spain, Holland and many other countries. Now, this ever-popular book has been updated for the 1990s. Much, of course, remains the same. Dads remain pre-occupied with work, whether it's driving a truck, milking the cows or dashing off to a new world of computers. And their traits show a remarkable consistency – from their love of cars to their oft-alleged laziness around the house.

But, however busy they are, however pre-occupied with work, money, and supporting their kids, dads still find time for play, for a lesson in life, for a tickle.

You'll find lots of grammatical and spelling mistakes in the book. We have always felt it right to leave the entries just as we received them. So no prizes for finding "printers errors"! All the entries, together with their often very creative illustrations, are the genuine work of the children.

We hope you'll have as much fun reading the book as we've had editing it. If the book comes to you as a gift from your own child, we're sure he or she would endorse many of the things that are said. And we'll be surprised if some of the passages don't bring a lump to your throat. For the love kids have for Dad comes across loud and clear.

Richard & Helen Exley

What is a dad?

Fathers like to think they are responsible, dutiful, orderly and enthusiastic and they endeavour to convince their children of this.

Julia   Age 12

A father's shoulder is something to sit on when there is a crowd and you can't see.

Jacqueline Small

Dads are people who can sleep anywhere. Dad always asks how things went at school. Dad never likes to be disturbed in the midle of the news.

Chris   Age 9

Dads are people whom you can call nick names with out getting yelled at.

Peter Smith   Age 9

Edward Hiller   Age 7

Antony Masters   Age 5

Baldy

Fathers are sometimes thin on top and some are as borld as a babies rear end.

Dave Clark   Age 14

Because my dad is so bald, he says his hair slipped down onto his chin to make a beard.

Mark   Age 13

Thomas   Age 8

Behind the wheel

Dads drive too fast and get Tiketteded.

John   Age 12

Fathers always take very good care of their shiny cars, and seem to think that their wives will scratch them.

Emma   Age 10

Dads think that they are the greatest drivers in this world. They usually comment on woman drivers. Usually the women are right because they are naturally cautious and men have to show off. Please do not get the idea that I am a supporter of the militant feminists, nothing could be further from the truth. Anyway when I drive I will always be right.

Ovenden

My father finds faults about my mother's driving constantly. Go left, go right, your driving is too fast and too slow. But when he is driving he does the same things himself.

Farhad   Age 8

Money reminds me of Dad because He is an accountant. Paint reminds me of Daddy because he is usally panting the house. If I sea a crash It reminds me of Daddy driving The car.

Timothy   Age 9

Dalton   Age 9

Dad and the TV

A dad is someone who watches TV while he's sleeping.

Myrna Knutson Age 8

My dad watches TV when it isn't on.

Valerie Caplan

When my father comes home at night. After dinner he sits down and watches football, football, football. If you were to say the house was on fire while he was watching TV he would say "Thats nice".

Guy Zuckermann Age 12

Daddies are for yelling at you to leave the football game on the television.

Mothers are for yelling at your daddy to shut up and change the channel.

Rhoda Sampson Age 13

A Father is someone to watch tv with

Brett Hanson

Duncan Barnes   Age 8

Poor old Dad . . .

Dads are very good at working in the garage and messing the house up.

Joanne   Age 11

I like my daddy's poggy tummy
I like to feel it squige.
I like my mummy's poggy tummy
but its not as good as his
Bryony

My dad tries to play golf,
Trys to ski,
Trys to play tennis
But so far he just hasn't been lucky.
Philip   Age 12

My dad is strong.
He's always up to things he is.
He hammers his fum,
Once he hammed his fum
And he had to go to the hostpital he did.
Karen   Age 8

Dad gets your french homework wrong.
Dad sleeps in his armchair all Sunday.
Dad is someone who trys to explain how the
kitchen shelf fell down.
Dad fixes the car and then has to send it to
the mechanic to be repaired.
Dad had to walk five miles to school when he was
a boy.
Dad was almost picked for the Olympics.
Dad is always talking about how he's going to have
Solar Pannels installed.
David

Theodore Thomas

Lazybones

A dad is someone who says he will do something some time, but the time never comes.

John

My dad has a funny hobby which I think is being lazy.

James   Age 8

My daddy is lazy Because He always sits on his rear end.

Billie   Age 8

Dads are never working unless they are forced to by mothers.

David   Age 12

My dad believes in everybody doing their fair share. So that when we go into the living room after cutting the grass, we see him lying on the sofa and watching T.V.

Julie   Age 11

When my mommy goes out my dad has to go to his mommy and have dinner!

Jason   Age 9

A dad is someone who will finish making a cupboard in the year 2000!

Joyce Blair

Some typical dad's talk:
"I'll fix the door tomorrow."
"But the hardware store's shut."
"But the ladder is broken."

Genevieve

Bruno Orsini   *Age 13*

19

Michael
Hellicar
Age 8

In praise of dads

In my opinion a father is a 'VIP' in his family!

Laura Antonucci   Age 11

My father is someone who makes me feel like John McEnroe if I get a service in.

Scott Strong   Age 11

What I like best about my dad is that he is proud of me when I do well in class, and even when I do badly he is still proud of me. I love him for that.

Anjanee Bissessarsingh   Age 10

If I didn't have Pa I think the world would be grim. He always help me with mi multiplications.

Darrell James

Dads love you more than anyone.

Claire Powell   Age 9

Father

Somebody that I
Can come to when
I'm sick
Worried
Wrong
Somebody that
Can tell me the
Solution
To life
AND
Progress;
And give me
HOPE
To go on.

Helen Holm   Age 10

Ali Abbas
Hanif   Age 8

21

Thank Heaven for dads

Dads usually ask you if you have had a nice day at school or wherever you have been. They are very busy people but they are never too busy to give you a kiss.   Katharine Rule   Age 9

Thank heavens someone invented dads.   C Matthews

My father sometimes cooks a fantastic chicken dinner. My dad tells me that he loves me very much. Dad made the family a fish pond. My dad is a carpenter. Dad makes all our cupboards. Dad made me a dollshouse and Dad is very kind to me. Dad buys me chocolate everyday and I love Dad very much.   Barbara Webb   Age 9

I like my father because he is always ready to listen and help me out of my troubles, big or small. He takes care of me and treats me well. He does not hesitate to give me something when I ask him for it. My father helps me when I am doing something difficult, and I always feel safe and sound when he is around. I think my daddy is my best friend.
Maltie Maraj   Age 11

A dad is a comforter. He comforts my mother when she can't reach her dreams. He cares fer us when she is upset or even mad.   Margaret   Age 12

My father is very funny and very pleasant. When he comes back home from work and is very tired, he cheers up as soon as he sees us.   Nadia Caraccio   Age 12

But seriously, I think dads are one of the most important assets a child can have. Don't you?   A McAuilhin

Good old Dad. He is adorable.   Antigoni Kalodiki   Age 14

Hayley   Age 8

I want the whole world to know my dad is very nice and kind to me.

Sharon Chapler   Age 10

The breadwinner

A dad is One of the most Important people in a family because he helps mom to earn money to keep the whole family living. So that means that a father is some-one who Cares for you. A father is a thing that you depend on.

Simon M Leese

A dad is a person who puts a roof over your head.
And who gives you a nice warm bed.
A dad is a person who works hard.
And on the weekend he spends his time in the backyard.
And puts food on the table for you to eat.
And puts shoes on your little bare feet.   Lisa Ann Millett   Age 11

After his breakfast away he goes to do what he needs to do for us. Don't know what he does, but in the evening, when he gets home his face is tired. Sometimes he comes home at lunch, and the talk is full of his meetings with strange people about strange things. The need for money, and those who suffer from the government. Land being taken over, or rents not paid.
This happens for the full week, but in the week-end he is different. Same bright eyes in a bright face, his black hair shining in the sun. He goes away to sail, one of his joys, and spends a day with friends and exercise. He is always changed after a break. Despite his office work, he is one who will always be with you.

Douglas   Age 12

Fathers are for earning money, so mothers can spend it.

Pam Munroe   Age 11

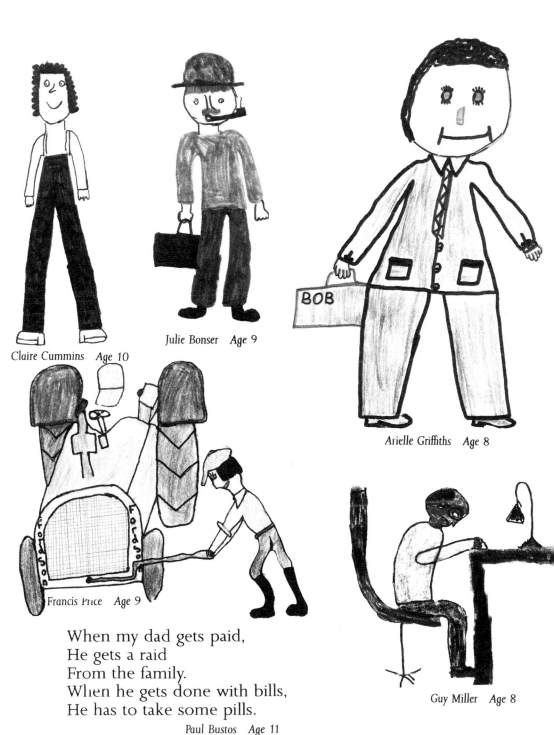

Claire Cummins   Age 10

Julie Bonser   Age 9

Arielle Griffiths   Age 8

Francis Price   Age 9

When my dad gets paid,
He gets a raid
From the family.
When he gets done with bills,
He has to take some pills.

Paul Bustos   Age 11

Guy Miller   Age 8

Life without them

I feel sorry for all the orphans all over the country without dads to look after them.

Brian Whitney

I don't know what I would do without my dad I would not have any Cristmas presents No birthday presents No food no shelter No were to live No nothing.

John Seane   Age 9

We're lucky to have a dad. With no dad we would have no food, no home. If people had no children the world would have no people, no heros, no heroines.

Ryan

I think really dads are a nuisance but you can't do with out them!

Paul

David Fraser

Sarah Galant

29

Caroline Greenwood   Age 8

A very happy mother
A very happy father
is what A family
should be like   Tracy Hampton   Age 6

30

Dad is away

My mother goes quietly up to bed,
I start to think of the tears she might shed.
Dad has gone and we're alone,
To live in this house of cold stone.
And he won't be back for another six months.

Dad is away on business,
The house is in a complete mess.
She does not seem to care,
About the house or what she'll wear.
She is very pretty my mother is,
But she looks untidy by wearing shirts that are his.
I wish she would tidy herself up.

Dad is coming home tomorrow,
Now there will be no more sorrow.
It's nice to see mommy happy again,
I can see a tremendous change.
It's great having him home.   *Angela   Age 15*

James Beasley
Age 7

What are dads for?

Dads are for giving you money, being boss, gardening, fishing, shooting, and any other pleasures that they can think of; that includes sleeping under a newspaper and pretending to be reading it.

Deborah   Age 13

In the home a dad is very important. He is the person who helps to provide us with money to feed and clothe ourselves. He can paint your bedroom, fix your radio, makes cages for your pets, repair a puncture in your bicycle and help you with your history homework. A dad can be very useful for taking you in the car to and from parties, music lessons, and dancing lessons. A dad is the person whom you ask for extra money. He is the one who complains about the time you spend talking on the telephone, as he has to help mom pay the bills. A dad is someone who will support you in an argument if he believes you to be right. He is someone who hears about your school results, and treats you if they are good. A dad likes to come into a nice happy home in the evening, and settle back in his chair with a newspaper. He likes to recall his Army days. On your wedding day he is again very useful, as he is needed to give you away. Although dads do not show it, they worry about you an awful lot.

Beverley Wilkins   Age 13

*Charlotte Hansen
Age 8*

A father is for staying home to be with his son.

Robert McConchie   Age 12

Dads are helpful and in every way,
They are not only there to do your hair
But to undo sticky problems.
That's why Dads are there.   Sarah Edworthy   Age 11

A dad is:
Someone to read you a bedtime story
Someone to have a fight with
Someone to burn the toast
Someone to go out with your mother.

Sara   Age 9

Dalton Exley

My Dad's working and he does the house chores. He tells you things that make you laugh. He buys you things for Christmas. He takes you for rides in the countryside so you should think kind things. He smacks you and teaches you and puts you to bed.   Darren   Age 9

Fathers are for erning money and helping to keep the human race going.

Susan Abbott   Age 10

35

Being with Dad

Now dad, he is the nice guy,
He'll sit and watch TV
And sheer bliss are the evenings
When I'm sitting on his knee.   *Susan Harvie   Age 10*

As a small child, I will always remember our family sitting beside a roaring fire in the living room, intent on our father as he read to us, the curtains shutting out the black night.
Elisabeth Cowey   Age 13

A father is a person who you love very much. He is never tired of hearing your jokes.   *Eduardo Vivo   Age 8*

My house is lonely when my father is at work.
Clara Ortega   Age 8

I like my daddy.

Richard de Cesare

Ferhan Kurtulmus   Age 9

Kung fu dads

I like my dad because he fights me. Darren P Griffin *Age 7*

My dad holds me by the middle, and says one, two, three. He pretends that he is going to throw me out of the window, but he realy throws me on to my bed. My dad runs up stairs pretending to be a monster. Nicola Jane Hickson *Age 8*

When dad wakes me up I usually burrow under the covers, because he turns on his radio and puts it on my ear. Then he tickles my feet when I turn upside-down. Charles Dornton *Age 11*

I like my dad when I have a fight with him. If he does not I call him an old man and he starts to chase me around the house and garden. Stuart Hughes *Age 9*

My dad is the kind of person that does Kung Fu on me and pulls me out of bed with a Kratie chop. Every weekend he gets my big brother to teach me how to kick my dad back. Andrew Pinder *Age 10*

Fathers are people that will fight with you but not hurt you. Christine Johnston *Age 11*

Harold *Age 9*

Saturday morning

The thing I like about my dad is he is very cuddly and soft especially on Saturday morning. I always creep in and snuggle up to him.

Suzanne Pinder

On Saturday morning my mother is marvellous. Out of bed she jumps (well, not exactly jumps) but she gets out of bed and down to the kitchen she goes tiptoeing, where she begins her wonders, bacon and eggs, sausages and tomatoes, beans (on special days) toast and a great cup of coffee for breakfast nothing burned (usually).
Meanwhile Daddy is still fast asleep, but as usual his bliss is ended by the four of us jumping on his bed waiting for one of his fantastic stories. I find that Daddy's stories are marvellous, they are exciting, frightening, amusing but above all imaginative. He is very good at those stories (Daddy made) but he always stops when there is a slight hint of breakfast, I wonder why? Daddy (I suppose) is patient, strong-hearted and above all kind. He protects all of us like a shepherd guarding his sheep (he even bleats, that is snores). He is tall, dark and handsome and though he is not fat he eats quite a bit. My mother never eats anything (she saves it all for Daddy) which he likes.
I don't know where I'd be if my dearest mother and father weren't by my side.

Belinda Scarborough   Age 12

Graham Weiss

39

Fun and games

My daddy lays on the floor and me and my sister get on him. We pretend he is a donkey.

Susan Lamb   Age 5

My dad is brilliant but lazy too because he always stays in bed when I am up. I like it when Dad lays on the floor because when he is not watching I sit on his tummy and start thumping him but he says it does not hurt him.

Amber Macdonald   Age 10

My father does sports with me even though I get hit by a softball cant reach a basket in basketball and kick balls into the woods in football. I still think it fun.

Andrew   Age 8

One of my dad's main pleasures is his golf. He plays in a local team all through the summer. He has the fanciest miss I've ever seen.

David

He helps me ride a bike

Rosa

A dad is someone who on the only day he doesn't work takes you swimming.

Elisabeth Fenton   *Age 12*

Andrew Green

Dads have hairy legs and big knee caps. Dads play with you and put you on their backs and toss you off and play tag with you.

David Owen

In the snow dads always pull you along on the sled, and they put up a good snowball fight. If you go out with your dad you can guarantee that you have a good time. Dads always seem to make things fun.

K Abele

Father can be a playful fellow. He'll tell the little children in the house a joke or two to make them jolly, to make them happy, merry children instead of miserable grumpy ones. That's what I like.

Jemima   *Age 7*

The things children say

One day my dad got married to a lady, her name was Elaine. Then they went on a honeymoon and they had a baby boy. His name is Brian but they had another baby, when they came home. It was a little baby girl. Its name was Sherry. After a couple of weeks my mother had me and she named me Rebecca.

Rebecca   Age 9

I found out about Santa Claus when Dad dropped all our toys on the wooden floor outside my bedroom and from then on I knew why my mother always put beer out for Santa, not milk.

Andrew Simpson

But one thing is my dad will not hit my mother he says if a man hits a woman he is weird. We say he won't hit her as she can hit harder than him.

Christopher   Age 14

My daddy has naughty habbits they are, Daddy says that Mommy has got is Keys but Mommy says she hasn't and Daddy says she has so Mommy says Look in your pocket so Daddy looks in his pocket and all that time he had them in his pocket.

Tracey   Age 8

My dad has a habit of buying my mother chocolates and eating them himself.

Craig Cohen   Age 9

A dad is a male mate to a woman. They buy a new house. And then they babysit their new children.

Erika   Age 12

Tina Vowles   Age 5

Joanne Rudge

My mother likes to have babies, but my father doesn't like to have babies.
Paul   Age 8

My daddy is funy He has false teeth and wen He gos to Bed He puts them under the Bed and wen my mommy gos to Bed my daddy false teeth Bits my mommy and she jumps out of the Bed.
Mary   Age 7

New dads always take on a smug self-satisfied expression of haven't-we-done-well, and they love having their little Achievement admired. But once the little achievement learns how to a) bawl incessantly b) ask for money and pull tablecloths from tables – "like the man did on TV" – their faces change to an expression of why-did-we-bother.   Lorraine Phelps

I think a father is a human being who watches you grow up into his little girl. Then he has something to brag about to his friends.
Debbie   Age 11

He sends us to school just because he want us to learn how to be a nice respectful gentleman
He punishes us for our sake and at first I sometimes get mad then I realize.
Samuel Lin

Nicholas   Age 8

50

On the warpath

When dads lose their temper, They go red, then purple, then red again.

Paula Age 11

Dad sometimes has bad days, so we try to be good and quiet.

Sally Age 11

When Mother's in a temper you're shouted at. But when Father's in a temper you're in for it.

Simon Age 11

When my dad is in a bad mood it isn't the most pleasant ordeal for who he's in a bad mood with.

David Age 11

When my dad gets very mad he kicks the doors. When my dad's in a good mood he goes out for a drink.

Alex Age 11

He's the good shepherd watching o'er you now, though when he smacks you its "Ow, ow, ow."

Sally Age 13

My dad says that sometimes I'm very bad. But I bet that my dad was *always* bad when he was small.

Celia Age 9

Dads grow big hands to spank people.

Scott Gallagher Age 8

Money

Dads are like moving banks.

John   Age 11

I don't get much money I think there should be a law that you double your child's money or else you have to go to jail.

Debbie

My father is a sport fanatic, especially for football. In the evening if his team has lost he is gloomy and down-hearted. When it wins he's glowing with excitement; now is the time to ask for that extra money.

Fiona   Age 13

My dad is a cop but even so my dad still sneaks money out of my mom's purse.

Mandy

When Dad comes home from work he likes me to give him a big hug and I do, especially on pay days.

Kristin

Lincoln   Age 10

Every week Dad gives me too little money. How am I supposed to live with inflation?

Kelly

Judith Gracie   Age 10

Mark Perrin   Age 9

My dad is the biggest teaser. But his kindness changes everything.

Jane Livermore   Age 11

My Dad is a softy,
he does tell me off sometimes but he makes a weedy effort.

Sam Mcrory   Age 9¼

My daddy is like clay, he is all hard and gritty, but when we do something like sweep the floor he goes all soft and smiley.

Gemma   Age 11

I like my dad because when he tells me off he says it in a soft deep voice and I don't feel hurt at all.

Tracy Sims   Age 9

The trouble with my dad is that he is ether mad or soft and nice.

Guy

My dad is quite nice if you approach him okay.

Fiona

In the eighteenth century a father was hard on the outside and inside. By the twenties he was hard outside but soft inside. Nowadays he is soft both outside and inside.

Mark

Tanita Montgomery   Age 10

59

Nothing but love

Parenthood is serious business.

Aysegul Corekci   Age 15

A man becomes a father only when his wife gives birth to a child. Till then he is only an ordinary man. When a man becomes a father he becomes the most responsible man on the earth.

Sandeep Sampat   Age 16

My father is happy but he sometimes sits on his chair looking sad and would not part from us for all the riches in the world.

Judy S Garcia   Age 9

When we get a big job we must not forget them because when we were small they did not forget us. When they are old and sick we must not leave then as strangers.

Michael M Rambert   Age 11

Big, strong athletic
Shrewd, just, understanding
Loving, fun, dependable
Always busy with business.

Evan Green

John-Paul Haigh   Age 8

Euan Leckie   Age 7

Some dads give them everything except love, some give them nothing but love.

Aysegul Corekci   Age 15

I call him a real dad

I love you because you are always there for me and you always love and care for me.

Lisa Weintroub   Age 11¾

To Dad

you are so special to me I think of you all the time you love me and I love you too. You care for me all the time you're there for me when I have problems thank you for being there for me.

Ruth Potts   Age 11

I wish for you a Rolls Royce car, and a luxury trip to France. I wish for you to be able to go to football matches or golf matches without having to look after me. I wish for you to be happy. I wish for you to have nice clothes and go out to posh Restaurants without costing you an arm and a leg. But most of all I wish you to have a good life without being stressed. I love you because you're the best dad in the whole world.

Danielle Green   Age 10

My dad's lovely he is just for me.

Mandy Tiwana   Age 11

God keep our fathers as nice as they have always been.

Jane Moppel   Age 12

Suzanne Causer   Age 6